NEW
LIFE
PSALMS

Poems And Praises
From The Trails Of A New Life

RONALD METZ

Olympus Story House
www.olympusstoryhouse.com

CONTENTS

PREFACE

Poems come in many styles and forms. They can be short or long, rhymes or cadences, and commercial or personal. To some they are an exercise in assembling words. But to those that long and listen for God they are love, knowledge, and wisdom.

Like everyone life is a journey. Knowledge and wisdom are seldom instantaneously acquired. Only on our individual paths of life with its trials, pains, and accomplishments do we grow. Then with our growing trust and faith in God the Holy Spirit provides the spark to create more than just words.

That love God gives brings life to words and songs so the heart can share what would have been unspeakable and unknown in other times. It cries out to be shared and praise God like the Psalms of the Old Testament.

Like building on Jesus' foundation to see more clearly God's creation and learn of His love with deeper reverence, joy and comprehension.

INTRODUCTION

Life begins and a world unfolds a world of choice and a world of possibilities to live in this world.

We all live a life and travel a path that is unique to everyone. To some it's a path lead near the home and for others a path traveling far. What each of us sees and how we perceive forms and directs our actions for life. Some never travel more than 23-50 miles from their birthplace and some cross the country or many lands. What we know effects what we do and how we interact with life, others and most importantly God. What seems to be overlooked by many is the relationship and interaction with God. God in our life reflects in our life with others and also their life with God.

Take the choice of paths and choice of voices to react and respond to, but who guides us?

We learn from the world and we learn from the Holy Spirit. The world is fickle and ever-changing, but not so the Holy Spirit. The Holy Spirit bids us to reason good from evil and calls us to reside with Him.

Paths, the paths we take walk alongside God or away from Him. There are no other choices. When we walk with God we sing, our life and our words.

But, it is a path and a growing process throughout our life and time. How do we see it and how do we share? We are taught by many in life. We are taught by what we experience and do. It could be a 10 year old in a Church play learning of love and caring. It can be through participating and learning in group organizations like Scouting, learning discipline, moral values, and teamwork. Participating in High Adventure camping at Philmont Scout Ranch, New Mexico, learning the personal limits and abilities as a crew travels the various terrains of hill and mountain.

We do not remain infants, when youth is passing into adulthood the learning never ends. Life and life with Jesus is never ending. There are times when the Holy Spirit causes us to overflow and share. Share the insights and teachings not just from the joys of life, but from the trials and hurts as well. The valleys and canyons that can seem hard and harsh, they were but a moment in time teaching us faith and endurance. Showing God's love and fellowship as He walks alongside, comforting and assuring us till we pass through. Then He holds us close refreshing, renewing and always ever loving.

The words that follow are Spirit and life. Guided, inspired and expressed over time. Like the Psalms of the Old Testament to praise God, express longing and desire, and share illuminations of life.

AWAKENING

CALL

I sit with tears
Stunned without words
Just incomprehensible sound
For words I've heard
To hear of life gone cold
An unfeeling shell
Divorced from caring and pain

What can life mean
To exist without dreams
To live without love for another
To live a good life for goodness sake

How Christ calls
How He pains for all to see
That life is love
And not just for me

He gave us His love
And He gave us a call
To love one another
To trust God's word and His love
To have faith in Christ Jesus
And live as His love

In His life He saw suffering
In His love He felt pain
In His compassion He healed them
Both the sick and the lame

They went without thank you's
They went without shame
They thought not of Jesus
Just themselves just the same
They turned from God's word

To their own tainted claims
They taunted and mocked Him
And laid on Him shame
He bore all their burdens
Yet He forgave them their blame

He calls on His faithful
To use Him as their guide
To show love and compassion
Through scorn and deride

Forget not the weak ones
The sick or the lame
And seek only Jesus
As solace and guide

For love is a caring
And Christ gave His all
What more we who follow
And answer His call.

ENCOUNTER

Encounter God
Face to face
In His Word
Know His love and His Plan

Encounter God
Face to face
Through His Son
Feel His love and His Grace

Encounter God
Face to face
With His Spirit
Grow in love and compassion

Encounter God
Face to face
With fellow man
Giving life we can treasure

Encounter God
Face to face
With our world
Show them direction, live with affection.

HEARTS

There are those of us in every age
That God has seemed to chose
For various and sundry tasks
Apart from mankind's use.

We read in books
And live in lives
That others might call dreary
But we've seen the son
And heard a call
The world just thinks we're silly.

Longingly we watch the sun
Rise and set in brilliant fashion.
And deep inside
With heart and soul
Is a flaming, yearning, passion.

To some we try to share it
To spark a fire inside
To some it remains sheltered
Lest their glaciered hearts collide.

PRAISES

I don't know where I'm going
I guess I never have
I think now I see God's plan
I see in there my potential
Its' time I said a prayer to Him
The maker of this land
I've worked so hard without Him
And I've tried my foolish plan
Now it's time I started to listen
And trust the Holy Lamb

It's time to give Him all my fears
And lay aside my plans
For God's pure and simple pleasure
Is to guide my very hand
He gives me music
And words to sing
Praises to my God and King
Praises to my God and King.

BEAUTY

BEAUTY

There's a beauty to watch,
There's a sight to behold,
They move through down low,
Or they move through on high.
It's clouds on the horizon,
They're moving past you,
Up in the sky.

They move with the wind,
O'er the earth, land, and sea,
And they travel to places,
That I'll never see.

Like the Lord,
Or a lamb,
Soft and gentle,
Come and stand,
Watch and see.
Like the Lord,
Or a lion,
Power and grand,
Bow down on bended knee.

They're moving and tender,
They're inspiring with awe,
They're white, soft like a feather,
They're black boiling masses,
With lightning and storm,
They're red golden masses,
Showing the light of the sun,
Let me be a cloud,
With the light from the Son.

BUTTERFLY

Moving here and moving there,
Like butterflies we are.
We travel on the Spirit's wind,
Traveling near and traveling far.
The butterfly is free to fly,
And spread its beauty over the earth.
And we can move and show GOD's love,
And the beauty of new birth.

ETERNITY

What was, is past
Eternity begins with now
Christ promised eternal life
Not someday, but from this day on

A gift from God you cannot buy
There's no way to even try
You cannot earn it
Only pass it on

Love and compassion show the way
He lives in us through the Spirit
And unites us with common bond
We live forever in a state of Grace
Eternal love, eternal grace.

GOD's BEAUTY

Flower bulbs and roots are like a man
Plain and ugly alone they stand
Given food and light in watered land
They soon grow tall and straight and grand
Like a canna leaves broad and strong
To flower stems and buds arise
The petals open and fragile vibrant beauty comes
Like translucent flames of orange and yellow
Softer than silk and cool to touch

Like the fragile spirit of a man
We root our hearts in GOD's commands
Like food for thought the Spirit waters the land
Our life grows tall and strong and grand
Nourished with Jesus in the heart of man
Our spirit blooms and shines to men
The translucent flames of love and caring
A soft gentle touch of care for others
Swaying lightly in the Spirit's breeze
Enticing others, with the fragrant scent of love.

GROWING

Flowers
Flowers live and flowers grow
From a tiny seed they start you know
People
People live and people grow
From a tiny egg they start you know

Small
So small
So quickly they do grow
Growing
Spreading
Reaching out to all
Budding
Blooming
Showing beauty to all

Infinite color
Infinite variety
No two ever the same
Growing
Blooming
Fading from our sight
The memory lingers
Forever beauty in our sight.

SPEECH

You saw two rainbows one summer night,
A moving show of God's great light,
It moved you so,
You wrote to me.
And there in words you expressed to me,
The wondrous detailed beauty there.
And though 300 miles apart,
God gave to me your wondrous sight.
I don't know how, I can't explain,
But somehow still I saw it plain.
I try to draw, I try to write,
So somehow more will see the sight.

TARRY

Winding through the valleys
The trail leads ever on
It passes streams and rivers
Which pool and then move on.

But farther up the trailhead
From whence the road begins
Winding through the hills
   and mountains
Journeys, begin and end.

Some travel on the byways
With blinders, straight ahead
Negotiating corners
And quickly moving on.

Others are too timid
And slowly travel through
Afraid that round the corner
They're travel may come to end.

Somewhere in the middle
On a peaceful steady course
Beauty is experienced
Traveling on this course.

It matters not the weather
That comes along the way
Or the seasons that are cycling
On an ever changing course.

Springtime brings a changing
Colors budding, springing forth
Blues and purples, whites and reds
And budding trees are everywhere.

In the summer trees are shading
In various hues of green
Reaching out and ever upward
With accenting colors all in bloom.

In the fall, colors are exploding
As greens turns to yellow,
   orange and brown
Leaves begin a-falling
To make a blanket on the ground.

In the winter, hills uncovered
Rocky patterns come into view
Rocks and hills framed by trees
And icicles grow into a
   blanket of snow.

The handiwork of God abounds
No matter when or where we are
The road goes on, the end in sight
Should I have tarried there?

CAMINO

Camino is short for Heartland Ecumenical Camino. This experience is derived from the original Catholic Cursillo movement, as are the Walk to Emmaus, Tres Dias, and many other spiritual renewal events. They are designed to bring a closer personal relationship with God and leadership to one's own church.

CAMINO

What is Camino?
Some say a Spiritual Renewal,
A call to live for Christ,
A call to work and serve our church.

It's all of that and even more,
Which tasks the words to tell.
For only GOD can show our soul,
The meaning of the walk.

We hear some talks,
And fellowship,
And eat and sleep a bit.

We pray to GOD,
And sing to GOD,
And stop to meditate.

Maybe it's the setting,
That brings the power on.
Or maybe it's the many things,
All rolled up into one.

The power's there,
The switch is on,
Feel the power surge.

There'll be some overloads,
But pop-off valves and crying towels,
Reside at every turn.

The call is out to see the LORD,
But he waits till we are ready.
There's no quick fix, no simple sign,
The heart will call when ready.

FLAMES
(for my wife)

While you're there at Camino,
And I'm still here at home,
A part of me is missing,
And it's hard to carry on.
It's the two of us together,
We're one though not in flesh.
I long to be there with you,
To fellowship with all.
It's hard to stay away from there,
I feel just like the moth.
I see the bright-lit candle,
And I want to come on in.

LOVE

(for my wife)

I hope I write for others
As well as I to you
We'll share our life together
Both happiness and pain
From birth to death
And all the pleasures in between
But this is one great pleasure
That I cannot give to you
No matter how the Spirit moves me
No words can ever speak
A far far greater love we have
Than I can even show
And each day at Camino
Is better than the last.

Snow

Camino is like snow
Unique as only GOD can create
Like a blanket spreading cross the earth
Protecting fragile plants from cold
Absorbed into the earth
Providing nourishment for all
Now looking even closer yet
I see each single flake
A complex fragile crystal
That man cannot duplicate
Each different and each beautiful
As only GOD can make
It matters not who you are
Candidate or Viajero
For each time that we attend
GOD makes a new flake fall.

CHANGE

CLOUDS

Tis the dawn of a brand new day,
Blue on the horizon after the gold fades away.
But here they come on silent wings,
Whiffs of white like cotton strings.
Then they grow like giant floating rocks,
A white and gray castle fortress grows.
As they grow gray turns to black,
A raging storm that blocks the sun.

Black and boiling masses collide,
Bringing flashes of lightning and thunder booms.
Raining, storming in its' wake,
Till winds die down and clouds begin to break.
Then peeks the blue through hues of gray,
And leads to sunshine and brighter day.

How so with men we start the day,
Till doubts and troubles cloud the way.
Growing, brooding dark and gray,
Anger grows blocking out the Son.
Words like thunder and lightning thrown,
Raining storms and hurt across the land.

The Spirit blows across clouded minds,
And clouded hearts begin to divide.
When the Spirit of Truth and The Son come through,
Our lives again with love will bloom.
Though the storms of life may cast a gloom,
The Love of God shines bright and true.
May the Spirit of God guide you each day,
And the Love of Christ be shown every day.

CONTROL

Control is not an issue
Control is a way of life
Whether we take it or leave it
Will form our very lives

Some will try to ignore it
Some grab it by the horns
Others run the other way
Like a summer thunder storm

Ignoring doesn't change it
But the horns can gore and scar
Man can't outrun a bull
And there's no shelter from the storm

The only thing we can do
Is use it as a tool
Hold it gently like a newborn child
Respect it like your dad

Share it with the ones you love
Don't hold it, like water behind a dam
Cause when the water gets too high
The dam is going to break.

FILL ME

Each of us was once a shell
Till the Spirit came to dwell
He fills our hearts
And touches lives
As no one earthly can
Feel the power
Feel the love
Move around the room
Soon you'll travel home again
To spread His love across the land.

TECHNOLOGY MAN

Technology Man
Robot with a living heart,
Walking, talking, facts and files,
Ask him 'bout a topic,
He'll tell you all about it,
He's read 'bout everything on file.

Technology Man
Robot with a living heart,
Never ever shed a tear,
Might stop his moving parts.

Technology Man
Robot with a living heart,
Ask him 'bout a topic,
He'll tell you all about it,
He's read 'bout everything of file.

Technology Man
He'll raise his kids up right,
He'll master the world,
   Go for the bucks.
What's for dinner tonight?

Technology Man
Robot with a living heart,
He's opened his mind,
With all that he's read.
But he's closed down his heart.
To the Spirit he's dead.

Technology Man
Robot with a living heart,
He's found the Grace
   he can't explain,
Now his life will never be the same.

Technology Man
Robot with a living heart,
He's changing parts,
He's living now.
He's left life's games,
Press reboot, begin
Now the living begins.

THE ROUTINE

Up in the morning
Off to work
Shoot an ugly glance
At some other jerk

Working 9 to 5
At the same old grind
Weekend comes just laying in bed
Livin out life with worry and dread

Then one day everything's changed
Up in the morning
Off to work
Share a friendly smile
At everyone you pass by

Working 9 to 5
Happy as a lark
Sharing love and kindness
In everything you do

Nothing changed but your point of view
Found a new reason
For getting out of bed
Serving the Lord Jesus
There's no need for worry and dread.

ETERNITY

Autumn Mist

Though the day's of life's autumn mists,
Have turned to dark winter grays.
Still the fire of Jesus love,
Warms and guides me through the haze.
And when at last the springtime comes,
And seeds sprout into blooms.
The Lord of love will garden here.
The Son shines down and waters, too.
To nurture summer crops till harvest's through.
Jesus still will guide me out,
To the shores of eternal home.

COMMUNICATION

Living through the ages,
Have we really changed
That much at all.
We started speaking man to man,
And painting on cave walls.
Everything that God spoke to man,
Was spoken rote to all.
Then we learned to carve in stone,
And manufacture paper and the quill,
But still the Word had not changed,
Nor will it ever still.

Doors

There came a gentle Spirit,
To dwell within my heart.
I came and opened up the door,
To welcome Him to my home.
As time moved on I closed the door,
And tried to go outside.
I traveled here, I traveled there,
And lo He came along beside.
The light shown out,
I began to see,
And lo I tried to hide.
The light shown on,
It's bright soft glow,
Became my comfort and my guide.
I've come back home,
And opened wide,
The shutters and the doors.
For all I want,
Is light right now.
And now, forever more.

HOUSE HUNTING

I went out around the town one day,
Looking for a house.
I looked and looked and looked some more,
To find the one that called,
And said "I am the one".
Some were big,
And some were small,
And some could house a band.
Some were plain,
Some were nice,
And some were very grand.
Some were brick,
Some were wood,
And some were hard to tell.
I looked at new, I looked at old,
And some were in between.
Some were hot,
Some were not,
And some sent shivers up my spine.
At last the harried agent said,
"You've seen them all my friend,
You've seen my list from A to Z."
The agent left but came right back,
With a puzzled look and said,
"You know that's strange.
An owner called and said come up,
He even asked for you by name."
So off I went to find the house,
Through the country all alone.
Down country lanes,
And gravel roads,
And then down a dirt and rock strewn trail.
Then there it was,
In a field of green,
With wild flowers everywhere.

Trees with upraised branches,
Towered up into the sky.
Squirrels and rabbits played nearby,
As deer and fawns looked on.
A contented peace seemed everywhere,
As far as I could see.
The house was built of native stone,
And each a perfect fit.
The wood that showed,
Looked old, but new,
Like somehow stained,
With a well-worn hue.
The man that came,
Was much the same,
A timeless face,
And an ageless grace.
He spoke with ease and eloquence,
My mind felt calm and peace.
He said "My son your home,
There's no more need to roam."
And then He said,
"This house for you, is free.
A gift for you from me."
Then stunned, I stumbling spoke
   "But why?"
He said, "No others heeded my call."
How much the Lord our God,
Would like to give His house.
And all we have to do is come,
And seek the route less traveled.
But how we wander here and there,
And seek all kinds of shelter.
When none will stand the test of time,
Except the Lord's peaceful shelter.

TRAILS CALLING

Another day
Another way
The trail of life goes on.

Along the roads of life we go
Our roads converge and flow
Each path we take
Is ours and ours alone.

God created each of us
With gifts and talents
Unique to each alone.

God made the paths
That we should go
And gave us choice
To stay or go.

To most of us
We come and go
On an individual trail.

But to some of us
We're called to join
Our individual trails
As one.

Like cords of rope
We're intertwined with God
For a strong and everlasting bond.

Together you will share
The strain of loads
That others cast aside.

The eternal strength of God
You share
Intertwined with love.

FAITH

ALTAR CALL

I stand before the altar,
Of the one true perfect GOD.
I sing before the altar,
To GOD and Christ above.
I kneel before the altar,
And pray through Christ's redeeming blood.
I lay bare upon the altar,
My joys and sorrows every one.
I work before the altar,
For Christ's with us everywhere.

DIRECTIONS

Where are we going
In this world today?
Where do our morals stand?

We arrest youths from gangs
For possession of drugs,
For rape and the theft of fellow man.

Where are the morals?
The love and compassion
That set man apart and above.

Where is our faith?
In whom do we stand?
In God, or some other man?

Can we love one another,
Like sister or brother,
If there's no greater love than from man.

The harder we try,
To show God's a lie.
The more we just prove His grand plan.

All nature cries out.
God's will, will out
Through Jesus, His Son, and our Lamb.

FREEDOM JOURNEY

I see the orange,
I see the blue,
The many colors, tint and hue.
All these things for man to see,
But even more for man and me,
Is God's great second sight to see.
It sets men free,
He carries our load,
And now we travel a different road.
So someday soon we'll travel on,
To God's own great and wondrous land.

PATH HOME

There's a man on a hill
In a dark and moonless night
Fighting off despair
With all his earthly might

Armed with a knife
It's a one man struggle
And a long way home

He's battered and bruised
From every trip and stone
He can't find home
Fighting all alone

There's an army of hope
Gathering in the glen
Nervous, anxious, waiting
For the signal to go in

Dawn is breaking
Driving gloom away
Light consuming darkness
Bringing calm into the day

Hope defeats the darkest foes
Dispelling worry and despair
Hope an ever present army
To show him the path home.

FAMILY

DAD

Dad you came into the world
You grew and took a wife
You loved for all your life.

Dad you brought us into the world
We grew and took out on our own
You loved us all you life.

Dad you lent a helping hand
To us and your fellow man
Your love will forever stand.

Dad you may have been just a man
But with love you'll always stand
A testament of God's loving lamb.

FATHER

Here it is.
It's Fathers Day.
But it's not the day,
It is the Fathers,
For whom the honor call goes out.

He loves his wife,
And helps raise the kids,
And works with fellow man,
But with Christ to touch his soul,
He moves to take a stand.

He lives to show a deeper life,
Of love for GOD not man.

He bares his soul and travels on,
Showing caring and compassion.
When others jeer,
He knows GOD is near,
With HIS healing for our lashing.

The road is long,
GOD shod his feet,
And gives him bedding in the grasses.

He seeks a meek and gentle life,
For his strength will ebb and flow.
Instead he shows the
    strength of GOD,
To conquer every foe.

And when he fails,
Christ hears his call,
And forgives him all trespasses.

He seeks not,
Man's glory or his fame,
For it will pass away,
Without eternal glory.

His fortune lies,
Within GOD's Grace,
Which surpasses human
    understanding.

MOTHERS DAY

Mother's Day's,
A special day,
We call to honor mom.
There's so much to say,
On one little day,
To honor each and every one.
They cook and wash,
Sew and mend,
And tend to household chores.
But that's not the really special thing,
That makes her special-ness.
It's the traits and special qualities,
That God instilled her with.
They feel our pain,
And soothe our wounds,
With compassion and with caring.
They offer smiles to brighten our day,
Like the shining sun,
And the springtime blooming flowers.
A careful touch,
Like a gentle breeze,
To calm and sooth the soul.
With patience through a trying day,
And loving words to help and guide us.
Mom's a special gift from God,
To teach and help and guide us.

SECOND PLACE

Through time and space,
There's just one place,
My heart remains besides with God,
That place I love,
And care for second most,
A place called family.
And even though I love my son,
Whom we've given back to God.
It's you, my wife, I love most here on earth,
As our two hearts are bound as one.

FRIENDS

ENDS

Living in strife
What a lonely life
Speeding on to a harried end.

For life on the edge
Is a perilous cliff
With a quick and tragic end.

What a change it would make
To change up the pace
And find a family of friends.

To listen to GOD
And commune with His Word
Find new rhythm and grace.

GOD gives us a time
To learn and to grow
And help others along the way.

Our love must be shown
Our community known
For this GOD has called all along.

FLASH, NOW AND EVERMORE

They say that dog is man's best friend
But really they are furry kin

We laugh and play
They lick and grin
They jump for joy
When we come in

If we cry or pout
They huddle close
To share the load
And comfort host

To scratch an ear
Or under chin
To stroke the fur
And calm the host

To laugh to love
To live a life
Growing closer
Each day of life

To chase a toy
Or rip open a wrapper
Make us laugh
And smile long after

When comes the day
The pain of passing
The heart is torn
Only love surpassing

The pain the loss
They linger on
Memories strength
Must carry on

Gift from God
Is dog to man
Love without words
Our furry kin.

PARTING

Shakespeare said, "Parting is such sweet sorrow",
How true then as well as in the 'morrow.
To each we have a life of love,
Of longing and of sharing,
For each of us we give a hope
With wisdom and with caring.
Following Christ who's gone before.

Although with change we're tempted,
With fear, and with questions.
Through Christ we learn,
To trust in HIS suggestions.

Our comfort comes from friends both here and now,
And from friends to come through Christ somehow.
Though we go on in time and space,
Through the Holy Spirit we're joined to this place.

SHARING

Here I stand with pen in hand
Rhyming words of prose
Few of which are ever seen
Just by my wife I do suppose
I seldom have a way with words
I usually pun around
But now the Spirit moves me
And I can open up
For greater deeper friends to share
A new and deeper life.

JOY

GOD's CALL

With hands anointed to God's call,
This cake was made for you.
It tastes like any other,
That you or I could make.
But the recipe is special,
Like grandmas used to bake.
I've worked on this for near 20 years,
And I think I've got it right.
With lots of hugs and wishes,
And an extra prayer or two.
Cause it's for someone extra special,
Someone who answers my GOD's call.

NOTES IN TIME

We are notes out of time,
Without reason or rhyme,
Till Jesus in our world does come.
With HIM as our staff,
We are one with a song,
And to HIS body of music we belong.
Let us be one in life,
As we sing through our strife,
Always knowing Christ by our side.

SOUL SONG

There's beauty,
In the way you sing,
And love comes,
To fill the air.
Let power come,
In words you speak,
And wisdom,
Stir the soul.

LONGING

LIFE'S ?

A million disappointments
A million lies
A million different reasons
To ask you why.

The hollowness is filling
I'm forming out a plan
Life can't move forward
Unless I take a stand.

The truth stands out
Truth cries out in pain
The truth is waiting
Patiently, quietly, restrained.

Truth can't be manufactured
To change what lies ahead
The past has changed tomorrow
By the truth of every word.

Man's arrogance
Constrains us
God's Grace and Mercy
Release our every pain.

Some say there's unity in sorrow
A vision through the pain
Only through reflection
Can we overcome the stain.

God calls us all in unity
To overcome the pain
Together we can be as one
Forever overcome the strain.

MUSIC OF LIFE

Life begins
We hear the call
A mother sighs
Her baby cries
A journey starts
And nature sings

The birds in the air
The beasts of the field
The forests' alive
With every living creature
The music of nature

Cycles of living
Cycles of growing
We feel God's song
And we sing along

One voice is searching
A chorus is stirring
Together a song
Grows joyous and strong

We live in God's presence
We long for His love
The music of life
We sing all life long.

SORROW'S SONG

My soul cries out in sorrow,
Oh, that I,
With one word,
Could end the torment.

Oh, that I,
With one breath,
Could end the pain.

Oh, that I,
Could send the signal,
That would end the sad refrain.

It cried aloud,
As my wife gave birth,
In those long and labored hours.

It cries aloud,
When I've hurt with words,
Or sided one with favors.

It cries aloud,
As my son endures,
The hurt and pain and dangers.

Now I feel,
And how I feel,
It causes me to tremble.

For how my God,
And my savior cried,
For all mankind's labors.

How much anguish,
Has mankind caused God,
Down through the ages.

And how much pain,
And suffering,
Did Christ partake upon the cross?

The bitter cup that I partake,
That causes me to stumble,
Is but a drop,
In a bitter sea,
That God partook for man.

Oh, sorrows' song a sad lament,
And revenges' joy is fleeting,
But oh, the joy of heavens song,
And the ecstasy of reconciliation.

LOVE

DEEPER

You ask me "Do you love me?"
I answer "Yes, I do"
Your question begs
Be more compelling
Than just a simple line.

The world around may advertise
And glamorize the body
But God made men and women
With a more comprehensive package.

The surface may arouse the senses
But the inner you stirs my soul
Many men seek shallow waters
Afraid to dive
And find the beauty below.

FIRE

Love is like a fire,
Glowing embers,
Rising flames,
Smoke and heated air.
Radiating warmth,
Reviving lives.

Can we fuel,
The fire of love,
And meet our God above.
Without the spark,
Of love that's His.
The Holy Spirit's wind rekindles,
Making embers,
Blazing fires.
Giving heat and light,
To all who pass nearby.

The heat helps prepare the food,
For others to carry on.
And by sharing love,
We fuel the fire to carry on.

So come on to my campfire.
Let's share the gift of love. Thanking
God for His undying love.

GOD'S TESTAMENT OF MAN

There are upon the earth today,
Two different kinds of men,
Those who walk with the Son,
And those who turn away.

It was a brisk winter morning,
And the clouds had cleared away.
As the earth lay before me,
Walking with my back to the sun,
I saw before me there,
The trees and all their branches,
Clothed in dark and somber tones.
Devoid of all their leaves,
They stand scraggly and bare,
Reaching out for something,
But never getting there.

Like life,
Lived on earth,
Without the saving Son.
Turn,
Now turn again,
And face the shining sun.

I see before me there,
As far as eyes can see,
The blinding crystal radiance,
Shining everywhere.
Trees and branches,
   grass and ground,
Wearing crystal robes,
Bowing down before HIM,

Humbled in HIS sight.
Bathed with the light,
Warmed with the fire,
Of GOD's loving hand.

I could stand for hours,
Marveling at the sight.
Grace and love abounding,
In every single sight.
The light of the Son is shining,
Through every single man.
With fellowship and caring,
In GOD's bright and perfect plan.

Harried

A harried man,
With a harried wife,
And harried children, too.
Moves along in a harried life,
Listening to what the world would do.

Abandon the fight
Let your feet take flight
From the world and its words of woe.

There's peace to be found
And much slower pace
When the Words of Our Lord be found.

Our burdens and cares
And our pains and despairs
Are lessened when we share the load.

God calls all our lives
If we'll listen and rest
On His Word, His Wisdom and Love.

LIFE

There's more to life
Than a Sunday Sermon
Sharing love and hope
Lighten load and blame.

See smoke and fire
Maybe a grand illusion
Sharing hope and faith
Rise above commotion.

Say you can't believe
Then what are you living
If God's not here
Then why are we living.

The future's now
The past's forgotten
Love is not lost
And never forgotten.

I'll live my way
But what's the cost
There's more to death
Than a heavy burden.

Where's the blame
If you can't live then
You can't live now
Show your love
And share your life.

LOVE

Love
Love for neighbor
Love of God
Protective love of mother hen
Nurtured love for next of kin
Growing love of man and wife.

Love's design
Love's fullfilling
Love's indwelling
Love's sacrifice
Love's forgiving
Love's more than feeling.

Love comes in gentle whispers
Love shouts aloud announcing gestures
Love's binding strength above all comers
Love's soothing touch calms the waters
Love's common place for excelling
Uniting hearts, embracing others.

LOVE'S STORY

God your love is so immense
It's difficult to fathom
You sent your Son upon the earth
Even though you knew the story.

I lost a friend I dearly loved
The grief still overwhelms me
The pain I feel as my heart explodes
Is so intense, beyond measure
And then I think of you O God.

For Jesus came and taught and died
And gave you praise and glory
You saw Him there upon the cross
How could you stand the pain it cost
To see Jesus die to fullfill the story.

MEMORY

Some say that it's amazing,
The things that I recall.
From history or the printed word,
Sometimes in great detail.

But oh, the memory like the man,
Is simple, yet complex.
I have a fascination,
With things upon this land.
But I can't go to the grocery store,
Without a list placed in my hand.

They say that within the mind,
Different sections are defined.
Some remember things for now,
And some remember for all time.

I may forget the grocery list,
But there's a blessing in disguise,
For if we have an argument,
And heated words exchange.
My attitude of love for you,
Will never ever change.

My memory's forgot the words,
That heated our exchange.
And all that's left is love and care,
For man to fellow man.
For Christ has brought this love to me,
And made my memory like GOD's slate.

NEW SONG

Smoother than wave washed sand upon the shore
Strands flowing like streams above
Like cascading falls upon the shores below
Undulating shores
Like the tundra of the North
Softer than the silken petals of the garden flower
Fragrant scent more lasting than a rose
Unique to only one
A gift
From God
You are.

STILL WATERS

Green grass and still waters,
Are waiting for you.
A cool gentle breeze,
And warm sunshine, too.
Lie back and relax,
As the Spirit descends.
And hear of God's love,
And the Word that He sends.

WINGS

As the mother hen protect her chicks
May the wings of love shelter me
The world around swirls like a raging fire
And running is my first desire
Let me climb the mountains
And see the depths
That only love can span
And finally leap on your command
As the spirit soars on wings of love.

PRAYER

ASKING

Every day of our life
We ask God for things
But do we give Him a reason for reply.

Would we ask it of others
Our wife, sons or brothers
Our parents or friends would we try?

When we receive gifts from others
Do we share our great joy?
Or do we tell them
"Thanks, now get out of my way."

If we care for each other
Our sisters and mother
How can we go on in this way.

Let us praise God on high
For His Son and His love
Let us give Him all honor and glory.

But if we stumble or fall
God's grace blocks the fall
For there's no end to His love and His mercy.

Let us fellowship there
And show all that we care
Ask for nothing but God's loving grace.

PATIENTLY

Patiently waiting,
Patiently praying,
That God's work
On our patient be done,
Let the healing be done,
As God's will be done,
And return us our brother in Christ.

TROUBLES

The troubles come
The troubles go
The Lord is there
Everywhere we go.

We grow each day
The more we pray
Our wisdom grows
Through God we know.

REDEMPTION

ARMOR

Once there was a man,
With a heart,
He did not understand.
So he stood alone,
He knew there was a GOD,
And Jesus was His Son,
But he failed to see,
What it meant to him.

He knew there must be more,
But he hurried with life's chores,
Never seeing pain.
Other's prayed for him,
And the Spirit worked within.
Now his armor's pierced,
And he lives again,
And he loves the Lord.

LITTLE BLACK SHEEP

Po lil black sheep, strayed away,
Done los in the wind and the rain.
"Oh hirelin, go find my sheep again."
But the hirelin say, "Oh Shepherd, dat sheep am black an bad."
But the shepherd, He act like dat lil black sheep wuz the onliest lamb he had.
And the shepherd went out in the darkness, tho the night was col an bleak.
An dat lil black sheep, he fin it, an he lay it agains his cheek..
But the hirelin, he say, "Oh Shepherd, don't bring dat sheep to me."
But the Shepherd, He smile, an he hold it up close.
An dat lil black sheep, wuz me.

Paul Lawrence Dunbar
circa 1900

Po lil black sheep
He's no longer lost or alone
The Masters done found him
And taken him home
He's dancin in heaven
And bowin at the throne
He's standin with Jesus
Singin us home.

Ronald P. Metz
September 22, 2001
Memorial for Don Bristow

QUESTIONS

Who guides the shepherd who lives in the field?
Who calms his fears as he sleeps with the flock?
Who comforts the shepherd at the loss of a lamb?
Whose voice does he answer?
Who lends him a hand?
Who fills his compassion?
Who lights the fire in his soul?

Who calls and convicts us?
Who mends all the pain?
Do we heed all the warnings?
That answer seems plain.
Can we find greater shelter?
Than the risen Son of Man?

REFLECTION

EXPLORING

Explore the mind,
Explore the heart,
Through all it's dark crevasses.
Look for life,
Look for love,
It's useless and it's futile.
Unless the Lord,
Will shine His light,
To show us through the passes.
His light goes on,
And in and through,
Until all eternity passes.

FORTRESS PLEASURE

Some men speak in angry words,
With nature's fire in heart,
They've closed their minds,
Their heart and soul,
Except to Satan's side.

They want this world,
It's toys and power,
It's useless, priceless, treasures.
The only thought and goal in life,
To build up 'Fortress Pleasure'.

But if they'd stop the great charade,
And useless mounds to treasure,
They might perchance begin to see,
A wondrous golden grandeur.

A crimson sky where eagles fly,
An emerald pasture meadow,
A crystal creek with bass and trout,
The woods with flowers blooming,
The doe and fawn that jump and play,
With hare and fox abiding,
Year by year they stand renewed,
God's testament of glory.

We see God's love for land and beast,
His caring and compassion,
And love for men,
Through Jesus saved,
His greatest moving story.

GIVING

What of the man,
Who gave till he's gone,
He gave wisdom to the fool,
Knowledge to the uneducated,
Love to the unlovable,
Sight to the blind,
He gave words to the dumb,
And sound to the deaf.

GLORY OF GOD

See the glory of God,
From a mountain peak,
In a crimson sunset,
On an autumn morn.

Hear the glory of God,
In a gentle breeze on an open meadow,
In a gentle breeze through a wind chime,
In an orchestral recital.

Smell the glory of God,
In the new mown hay,
In the kitchen with fresh baked bread,
In the blooming walk through a formal garden.

Feel the glory of God,
In the touch of a flower petal,
In the stroke of a cat's fur,
In the touch of a newborn child.

Show the glory of God,
As the Holy Spirit moves within.

Harvest Time

Here come the Pharisees
Lookin out for heresy
Judging by what the law allows.
Lookin over you'n me
Could that be a speck, I see
They won't even give you time.
Decked out in finery
Making fools of you'n me.
Just you wait till harvest time
There's a giant load of logs to haul.

INSTRUMENTS

I am a living instrument,
Which the Spirit moves at will,
Though time and man's intelligence,
Try to fool us with self-will.

LABYRINTH

God's designed a single path
A course through time and space
A labyrinth of love and grace
To lead us through our life.

But here we are with axe and saw
Impatient, barely waiting
Cutting through and moving on
Till we're lost a-mazed and floundering.

We need to stop and wait for God
For time will pass and heal the wound
And the path will grow anew.

Then humbly, patiently we can move
And watch God's path unfolding
A labyrinth of love and grace
To bring us home again.

NOBODY KNOWS

Nobody knows me,
Like I know me,
But I don't know me,
Very well.

Nobody knows you,
Like you know you,
But you don't know you,
Very well.

How can I see,
What you see,
When you can't see,
What you really see.

How can I tell you,
Exactly what I'm thinking,
When I can't tell me,
Exactly what I'm thinking.

If my mind,
Were you're mind,
And you're mind were mine,
And together we need no words.

Only God can span minds,
Linked by the Spirit,
And share a life with Jesus,
Joined for all time.

PUZZLES

Take two rights
One must be wrong
Take two wrongs
Doesn't make one right.
If something's lost
How can it be found?
If something's destroyed
How can it be reborn?
If I cut a piece
To fill a puzzles void.
Can the puzzles image be restored?

RAINBOW SONG

There amongst the black and gray,
Storm clouds play and dance around,
Though the rain may fall,
And the land be blest,
God still shows the best for you.

With rainbow arcs of color,
   not one but two,
With clouds around with purple hue,
Make me stare with awed delight.

The outer rainbow arcs of lighter tint,
Call me in with a royal glow.
Inward now between the arcs,

A band of clouds with royal garb.
Though black and gray and
   fleecy white,
They're cloaked on top with
   purple light.

Inward now the inner rainbow arcs,
The brightest show of colors known,
Announce to all God's royal show.

And moving inward further yet,
With greens and blues to purple hue.
Fading softly the stage is set.

And there God's amphitheater sets,
With air so still it looks like glass.
There the mind can hear God's voice.

Speaking softly God to man,
Of promises, hopes, and plans,
I'd be there still, the admissions free.

But God has other plans for me,
My heart will wait for Him to
   come again,
Will you come too, and enter in.

See Me

Searching, waiting, dreaming
Don't want to seem scheming
Don't want to seem aloof
But don't want to seem self-serving
To seek recognition
To avoid sinful pride
On a tightrope I slide
Driven but dying inside
Weighing the balance of restraint and pride.

I want recognition
But at what price is fame?
Shyness or boasting
Which is greater or worse?
Can self-confidence fight doubt
Without destroying restraint?
Can fear of both destroy all?
Can quiet reserve seem aloof and repelling?
While silently crying for friends.

SEE THE CLOWN

See the clown,
The wisest of men,
He comes into town,
And all the children flock to him.

See the clown,
The wisest of men,
He acts out our lives,
We just laugh back at him.

See the clown,
The wisest of men,
He acts for the Savior,
Let's let Jesus come in.

See the clown,
The wisest of men,
For he takes off his face,
And only God can see in.

RELATIONSHIPS

AGES OF MAN

I think back through the ages,
How GOD's word has passed from
   man to man.
And look at how technology,
Separates Spirit and the Man.

At first GOD spoke directly,
To each and every one.
Then He sent the word through one,
And said to pass it on.

Then He put the word on stone,
And called us to come and see.
Then we went to paper,
And passed the word around.

Now we've gone electronic,
To speed through time and space.
But though we learn,
And build and grow,

It's to some away from God.
We forget the source, Of all
   great gifts,
And follow I, instead of HIM.

Oh, how the Spirit's blessed us,
With gifts to each and every one,
But how cold and callous can we be,
In treating fellow man.

God calls us to love and cherish,
To honor and to heal,
To trust and obey and go HIS way,
And love our fellow man.

Jesus made the sacrifice,
For each and every man,
And asked to take our burden,
If we would be HIS lamb.

Evangelism on the Bowling Lanes

Living for Jesus is like a bowling game,
We strive and pray to make a strike,
Each and every time we roll.
Do we stand firm on His word?
Do we follow through in His love.
God is a God of second chances,
Do we pick the others up?
Do we spare time to show His love?
Do we make the best of each and every frame?
We stand in the lane and roll the ball.
Do we show patience and persistence,
Through every frame?
And when we're done with each and every game.
Do we give God his due in glory,
Forsaking individual glory.
Do we play the game on every team.

LONELINESS

Lonely is a singleness,
An empty yearning void,
A burning want,
To fill the hull,
Of a crying hollow man.

We cry out in the wilderness,
We cross the burning shifting sand,
We turn ourselves inside out,
To find an answer if we can.

Some work and work and
   drive themselves,
As hard as they can stand,
Some run, or drink, or
   consume drugs,
In vain effort to fill the loss.

Others look within themselves,
For a lofty mystic plan,
Trying to delude themselves,
Thinking that I am.

Some look to companionship,
To fill their lofty plan.
All are lost within the void,
Of sinking empty sand.

For none have sought to
   hear the voice,
Of the one true great I AM.
He fills the void of emptiness,
He brings all men together,
His love is greater than us all,
It binds and pulls us all together.

For His love is the singleness,
That answers all the questions,
Of who and why and when and how,
Our life can have its' meaning.

PILGRIMS

We are pilgrims on GOD's Camino.
We have inherited a mansion
In the City of Light
And we walk the path
The Lord has chosen.

The path may be short or long
Or at times be rugged.
The Lord takes our burdens
As we take His yoke.

We must remember
We travel not alone
Others travel with us
They help us when we stumble
As we do for them as well.

How else could we share life's joy?
And look with wonderment and awe
At eagles soaring in the clouds
Beneath the mountain peaks;

At doe and fawn beside the brook
And playful dancing squirrels
At beautiful flowers all in bloom
And some of life's grandest perfume.

The silent calm of a babbling brook
The beautiful trout and salmon
There's a never-ending list of joys
And a never-ending challenge.

But how much harder would
    all things be
Without pilgrims to share them
So all the more I say to you
Come walk with me today.

And we will continue traveling
Down GOD's Royal Camino
Onward to the City of Light
To meet our Father in Heaven.

UNITY

Gas tanks on empty
Moving kinda slow
Going to make a Walk
Let the Spirit overflow.

Got a bigger family
In the house of God
Huggin and singin
Proclaim the Power of GOD.

The Spirit's going to join us
No matter where we're from
The Word of GOD will teach us
Each and every one.

Every road is different
But the end is still the same
And when we cross each others path
Rejoice we're all the same.

So I can call on you for help
And you can call on me
To share a life in Christ
And live in harmony.

REVIVAL

PRODIGAL

The Spirit moves around the globe
It's journeys to complete
It matters not just where we are
When the Spirit passes through
We stand before Him as linen
And He the purest cleansing bath
And when He's done we're pure and clean
Acceptable to the Father
Through Christ the Son
The prodigals return.

Rooster Calls

Wake up
The rooster calls
Wake up
A new day proclaimed.

Hear the call
A new day rises
Hear the call
Life begins anew.

The rooster calls
Jesus answers to us all
Live today
Spread the love that never ends.

Hear the rooster
Every day begins anew
Life with Jesus
Love that never ends.

Jesus is calling
Sending Grace throughout the land
Jesus is calling
The Shepard calls to all his lambs.

SEASONS

NASHVILLE CHRISTMAS

Drivin' down the interstate,
Fightin' all the cars,
Listen to the Opry greats,
Singin' to the stars.
It's a Nashville Christmas,
All across the land,
Listen to the country stars,
Sing the Gospel songs.
Praises to God on high,
Thoughts for fellow man,
Presents to exchange,
For God and fellow man.
It's a Nashville Christmas,
All across the land,
Listen to the Opry stars,
Sing with gospel band.
If I can't see Nashville,
At this Christmas time,
Let me hear the country stars,
Sing the gospel songs,
It's a Nashville Christmas,
All across the land,
As the Grand Old Opry Stars,
Sing the Gospel songs.

NURTURE

When Springtime comes and sprouts appear
The Lord of love will garden here
The Son shines down and waters, too
To nurture crops
Till harvest's through.

SEASONS

Though the days of life's autumn mists,
Have turned to dark winter grays,
Still the fire of Jesus love,
Warms and guides me through the haze.

And when at last the springtime comes,
And seeds sprout into blooms,
Jesus still will guide me out,
To the shores of eternal home.

Seasons Reward

Some say there's a doorway from summer
Down a path that's exceedingly long
They've forgotten they're on a journey
And who called them and walks on along.

When fall comes
And leaves start to falling
Think not of the journeys end
The colors changing is a signal
Of new life about to begin.

We've grown and stored up knowledge
That we must now pass along
For no one learns from tomorrow
To live out our lives today.

For knowledge saved is sorrow
If placed in hidden stores
And knowledge shared rejoices
As it grows like yeast in loaves.

We may not bend like saplings
But we've weathered many storms
Our roots grow deep with knowledge
And our fruits known far and wide.

A seed sown from our knowledge
May someday save a life
And that's how God intended
As we live through Jesus Christ.

So season after season
Each has it's own reward
But only if we share it
Can others know the Lord

SPRINGTIME

It's springtime in the city
And everywhere I go
There are cats and kittens resting
Taking in the show.

They sit among the flowers
Green but not yet bloomed
Taking in the sunshine
And watching every move.

As the gentle breezes pass them
Their sleepy heads nod along
In peace and tranquil beauty
In time with God's great song.

It's springtime in the city
And I am like the cat I stand in
God's great glory
And see his wondrous works.

I feel the Spirit move me
And I pray I move along
In peace and tranquil harmony
To follow God's great song.

TIME

A thousand years is but a day,
And a day a thousand years,
And I am but an infant,
In the days that pass away.
Oh, should I live a hundred years,
A child I'll still remain,
And should I live a thousand years,
I'll still remain the same.
What I know is as a child,
When seen within GOD's view.
Infinite in wisdom,
Patience, love, and care,
He calls me to abide with HIM,
Through Jesus we will share.

TREASURE

Pirates

High Ho,
Off we go,
It's a pirate's life for me.
Set the sails,
And man the deck,
We sail uncharted seas.
We're out for hidden treasure,
Whether buried, Or in the hold.
We'll move in fast,
And strike em hard,
Their burdens to relieve.
We'll set the slave and captives free,
And teach them all to sing,
Of the Spirit wind,
That moves us on,
To fight for Calvary.

THE POSTMAN

I'm just the friendly postman
That some of you may see
Walking down the byway
From house to house in town
I walk along in silence
A solitary stroll
But though the winter freezes
And the summers boil
Still the Spirit moves me
I've got to tend my sheep.

To many people all they see
Is a growing pile of letters
But there is more for me to see
While walking down the street
In spring there are the flowers
In fall there are the leaves
The sparrow wings and the robin sings
And more precious even yet
Is the rabbit huddling in the trees
And the children here and there
It causes my heart to soar
And more the Spirit moves me,
The friendly postman,
I've got to tend my sheep.

TRIALS

BURDENS ROAD

How many times have we walked the road,
In quick and easy steps,
And turned to find the road downhill,
And were nearly trampled by the masses.

But there's a trail up on the right,
That most have failed to take,
It's not the easy one some would like
They can't travel so heavy laden.

But had they gone on round the curve,
They'd find their burden taken.
For our guide resides upon the trail,
His home at the end is waiting.

His burden's light,
And He'll share the load,
Of those of us, heavy laden,
Who chose to take this road.

FALL

Lord, when all around me
Is gray and dark
And all I do is fall
I can't see the path to travel on
Or see where I've traveled from
Should I walk and stumble on
Or stop and crawl on hands and knees
If I stay will I go up
Or tumble, how long the fall.

Jesus Call

There's temptation and there's peril,
There's illness and there's strife,
As Satan tests our living,
In our faith in Jesus Christ.
There's Steven and there's Mark and John,
There's Matthew and there's Luke,
There are trials and afflictions,
On the traveled road of Paul.
Our bodies can be racked with pain,
Our spirit vexed and strained,
Because the source of which we fight,
Posses more power than we maintain.
We call upon the Lord to help,
His power conquers all,
And it comes in many guises,
Through one or help from all.
For others offer a source of hope,
They can comfort when they call,
For GOD's body of believers,
Is GOD's power source on call.
Satan tries us one by one,
The symptoms are seen clear,
The world around us boils and churns,
With his manifested schemes.
The answer is a call to arms,
GOD's body wages war,
For nothing's lost to Satan's fight,
If we answer Jesus call.

REMEMBER

Remember the mountain,
The beauty, the awe, the majesty,
Remember the mountain,
Only you know the experience you feel.
Remember the mountain,
There's a world full of sinners wanting to know
Remember the mountain,
Jesus is calling from the valley below.
Remember the mountain,
When trials bring you down.
Remember the mountain,
God's love never fails Remember.

SHOW TIME

At times it seems I'm standing,
While my mind runs in overdrive,
With a hundred different things to do.
And no resource for even one.

My frustrations not with anger,
For there's no one to place the blame.
It's a helpless lonely yearning,
With a passion to make a change.

I know
That I can't change the world myself.
With
Or without money.

But I see around me,
Things that could make others grow.
I see the things that could help save lives.
But I don't see others helping.
Instead they turn and close their eyes.
And quickly pass on the other side.

Can I pass this love from man to man?
Can my love forever grow?
Will you meet me at the junction?
And help my Jesus show?

THE STAGE

If all the world's a stage,
Who's the audience to be?
Can I take part?
Yet watch the stage,
From sea to far off sea,
With fair impartiality.

If all the world's a stage,
Then who directs the acts?
Who sets the lights,
And builds the stage,
Which changes constantly.

If all the world's a stage,
What kind of play are we?
Is it an ever-changing drama,
With sorrowful notes of tragedy,
Or laughing comedy.
I sometimes get my lines mixed up,
And sometimes I hate the part,
But the playwright comes,
To guide my soul,
To encourage and to guide.
He sent His Son to play the lead,
And His Spirit is my prompter guide.

If all the world's a stage,
Let's all the playwright praise.
He wrote each scene,
He choose the cast,
He writes the lines for me.
How can I not give all my best,
For the playwright is my audience,
And to please Him is my goal.

WAVES

I heard the man,
Stand up and say
"Me, I'm a self-made man,"
Others stood and sang his song,
And others cheered him on his way.
All I saw were weak, blind, stumbling men,
Swimming farther out from shore.
Some rode high upon the sea of pride,
While others sank below the wave.
They could have turned back to land,
But the waves all blocked their view.

UNDER THE BIG TOP

All the world's a stage,
And a troupe of fool's are we,
We juggle time and emotion,
We walk high wires of fear,
We dodge the dancing elephants,
That would press us to the ground,
We tame the friendly lion,
With a chair and cracking whip,
We charm the deadly cobra,
Till he falls back in his pit.

Through it all we wear a costume,
And make-up a happy face,
Inside we're nearly dying,
With quaking boots and shaking hand,
Remember always through the danger,
God's safety net of love,
He's mending hearts and saving lives,
Through Jesus Christ, His Son,
The Holy Spirit is the Ringmaster,
And The Word our safety guide.

TRUST

God's Hand

I'm tired of fighting battles,
Elijah, come and show the way,
Let's run into the mountains,
And escape from tragedy.
I want to sit in the mountains,
And see the day turn into night.
I want to see the guiding light,
Piercing through the dark.
I want to wait and sit right here,
Till Your gentle breezes blow.
I want to see Your works O Lord,
And hear the Spirit sigh.
I want the comfort only You can give,
No matter how much time goes by.
Your hand is always here to guide,
Though weary I may be.
Your love to me you kindly show,
Through Your eternal loving Son.
I'm tempted still by love and hate,
Through Your power give me strength.
For me alone I cannot stand,
Unless I have Your hand.

SAIL ON

I'm constantly divided,
As the world I roam unfolds.
My ship sets at anchor,
Until the falling sail unfolds.
I'll perish here if I remain,
But which direction shall I go.
The current begs me travel in,
The wind says travel on.
The other ships have traveled in,
And some are in the bay,
But others sit among the rocks,
Or to pirates fallen prey.
But should I chart untraveled seas,
And travel on alone,
With only words to guide me,
Into the vast unknown.

The current is technology,
With the ever changing tide.
It moves in unseen silence,
Or with fury crashes land.
To some who are unsuspecting,
Are crushed upon the rocks of time.
To those who are not ready,
Are abandoned on the sand.
And those that reach the quiet shore,
Are passed by in the night.

The wind's the Holy Spirit,
Moving on as God would guide.
It helps us cross the tide of time,
No matter where the current flows.
Should I try to get there.

With the oars I've stored on board,
I'll soon be lost within the tide,
A nervous tortured wreck.
To place my faith in Jesus, Lord,
And with the Spirit sail,
It brings me comfort,
Brings me power,
To move me on,
Toward God's appointed goal.

SPOKEN

GOD spoke upon the void
And created sky and all the masses
GOD breathed upon the land
And created lads and lasses.

GOD spoke with us face to face
That we might join with Him
In fellowship as companions.

GOD spoke to us to hear
We listened not and fell away
GOD's heart was sadly broken.

GOD yearns for us
As parent for a child
Who's lost along the pathway.

GOD searched for us
We thought it fun
To hide among the grasses.

But GOD can see
The danger there
A snake among the grasses.

Can we listen now
The Father calls
He'll save us from the viper.

If we'll return
We'll miss the fire
That clears the land
And starts anew the grasses.

To Learn

I came to learn the Word of God,
From those who know a lot.
I learned of law and sin and then,
I listened to them not.
I came to learn the Word of God,
From those who knew not what.
I learned of man and self and then,
I turned to hear them not.
I came to learn the Word of God,
From those who know the lost.
I learned of love and sacrifice and then,
I became one among the flock.

TRUST AND INNOCENCE

There is a little kitten,
That brightens up my day.
And each day that I pass there,
He wants to run and play.
He can't talk or speak a word,
But still he shows his love,
With a purr in his throat,
And a look in his eye,
He shows his warmth to me.
All he asks is love and care.
A simple life of trust and innocence,
That kitten shows to me.
Is like our life in Christ,
And the love our Father shows.

WALLS

There's a place in California
That's been sung about for years
Its windows may have beauty
And its doors are never locked
But the walls that build
And surround it
Are dug with a heavy heavy cost.

Though the Chapel has such beauty
And a quiet serene peace
Few will come to see it
Without heavy bonds and chains.

They come to serve and toil there
And many never leave
It's the Gray Stone Chapel
Within the Folsum Prison walls.

How many are we Christians
Bound with heavy chains of sin
Living in our Grey Stone Chapel
Locked away in prison walls.

We dig from the Words of the Bible
And build up fortress walls
To keep the world around us
From entering into our stalls.

Jesus broke what binds us
And freed us from our stalls
But yet we linger
And build up higher walls.

We call the world around us
To come and see the halls
But they are loath to travel
Into the dark foreboding walls.

Unless we travel out to them
And bring to them our light
They'll never know the love
  we've found
Through Christ's forgiving Grace.

If we can't go into the world
And bring the peace of Christ
All they'll see are prison walls
And dark foreboding stalls.

BIOGRAPHY

Born and raised in Winfield, Kansas and participating in Cub Scouts, Boy Scouts, and Explorer Scouting I learned not only camping from overnight to ten days at Philmont Scout Ranch, New Mexico, but devotion, duty and teamwork.

I have spent over twenty-two years in the U.S. Army, from the Kansas National Guard to Active duty and U.S. Army Reserves. From being an enlisted member earning the Good Conduct Medal to an officer receiving the Distinguished Military Graduate from ROTC and Honor Graduate from Field Artillery Officer Basic, Signal Officer Advanced Course and Quartermaster Logistics Courses. Additionally, I have received the Army Achievement Medal twice, the Army Commendation Medal and a Letter of Commendation (for writing a computer program).

I worked more than twenty-five years as a letter carrier for the U.S. Postal Service in Joplin, Missouri, retiring one month after the F5 tornado destroyed 6000 homes and businesses and killed 161 people. My work has allowed me to witness life in all its forms—people in motion, fleeting moments of kindness, and the quiet whispers of God's presence.

Additionally, my experience as a trained clown and balloon artist has given me a deep appreciation for joy and connection. Life is a continuous learning process and does not end and in 2013 while studying Business Management at Crowder College in Neosho, Missouri I participated in the Future Business Leaders of America National Convention and placed 1st in Business Management Concepts competition. Now retired and living in Cookeville, Tennessee, with my wife of over fifty years, I remain dedicated to sharing my faith and insights through my writing.

www.ingramcontent.com/pod-product-compliance
Lightning Source LLC
Chambersburg PA
CBHW021648120626
46545CB00002B/764